They're Tearing Up Mulberry Street

BY YVONNE NG • ILLUSTRATED BY RICHARD SMYTHE

amicus ink

Mankato, Minnesota

For K.P. with love—Y.N.
For Henry —R.S.

Text copyright © 2021 Yvonne Ng
Illustrations copyright © 2021 Richard Smythe

Published in 2021 by Amicus Ink, an imprint of Amicus
P.O. Box 227, Mankato, MN 56002
www.amicuspublishing.us

Library of Congress Cataloging-in-Publication Data
Names: Ng, Yvonne, author. | Smythe, Richard, 1986- illustrator.
Title: They're tearing up Mulberry Street / by Yvonne Ng ; illustrated by Richard Smythe.
Other titles: They are tearing up Mulberry Street
Description: Mankato, Minnesota : Amicus, [2021] | Audience: Ages 4-7 | Audience: Grades K–2
Summary: "A boy walks home one day, only to find his street under construction! As he enjoys watching the excavators, bulldozers, dump trucks, pavers, and more, he gets a sense of the building process from start to finish. From blueprints to demolition to fresh, new asphalt, friendly, bright illustrations show the construction machines and workers up close"—Provided by publisher.
Identifiers: LCCN 2019050207 (print) | LCCN 2019050208 (ebook) | ISBN 9781681522388 (hardcover) | ISBN 9781681526560 (ebook)
Subjects: LCSH: Roads—Design and construction—Juvenile literature. | Construction equipment—Juvenile literature. | CYAC: Roads—Design and construction. | Construction equipment. | LCGFT: Instructional and educational works. | Literature.
Classification: LCC TE149 .N4 2021 (print) | LCC TE149 (ebook) | DDC 625.8/5–dc23
LC record available at https://lccn.loc.gov/2019050207
LC ebook record available at https://lccn.loc.gov/2019050208

Editor: Rebecca Glaser
Designer: Timothy Halldin

9 8 7 6 5 4 3 2
Printed in China

I was coming home from school,
skipping happily,
when a huge excavator
rolled down the street toward me!

But after enjoying this wonderful treat,
I saw they were tearing up Mulberry Street!

"This road needs help,"
the civil engineer told me.
"Cracks grow into potholes,
as you can clearly see."

"The sewer pipes are old.
The water pipes have lead,
and the street lights are dim,"
the engineer said.

The jackhammer busted the concrete into rubble
and broke up the road without any trouble.

The operator maneuvered
the excavator arm.
I watched behind the line,
far away from harm.

Then I ran home super-fast on my two little feet
to tell Mom what was happening on Mulberry Street!

The next day the excavator
had on its big bucket.
The operator used it to get
each concrete nugget.

The pieces were put in the dump truck with skill.
Another truck replaced it when the first one was filled.

SCRAPE, *CRUNCH*, **RIP**
went the machines' rhythmic beat
as they deconstructed old Mulberry Street.

When the old road was gone, the deep trenching started.
Holes for pipes were dug out, as the blueprints had charted.

The loaders brought pipes and long conduit,
and workers laid them down in the deep dirt pit.

Then they filled in the gaps
with clay or with sand,
and dumped two feet of soil
to grade out the land.

Tubes for water, poop, and light
now buried nice and neat,
will make homes fresh and bright
down on Mulberry Street.

Though utilities were connected,
the road wasn't done.

Dump trucks brought more
sand and gravel by the ton.

This structural layer will hold traffic weight,
like cars, buses, limos, and trucks hauling freight.

Bulldozers arrived to
reshape what was dumped
and rollers compacted
the lumps and the bumps.

The big machines all worked
like a slow-moving fleet,
to create a level base
for Mulberry Street.

Then big graders arrived
on their big rubber wheels.
They leveled the road bed
with a straight edge of steel.

With the base road finished,
the following crew
built the curbs and sidewalks
and put gutters in, too.

They built out wood forms
to guide the concrete flow,
which came down the chute
as a gloppy, gray dough.

The paver arrived
along with its crew.
Its heater then started
to warm up the goo.

Augers turned the goo out
while the screed pressed it flat.
Then rollers compacted it
down after that.

More asphalt was laid, made soft from the heat.
Layer after layer, they built Mulberry Street.

The finishing crew painted white and yellow lines, and then they erected new lights and road signs.

MULBERRY ST.

There it was, all reconstructed,
so nice and neat,
this fresh new road we live on
called Mulberry Street.

MACHINES ON MULBERRY STREET

Bulldozer

Excavator

Jackhammer

Loader

Paver

Roller

Job: Civil Engineer

Before construction begins, an engineer:

1) Meets with people living in the area and with city government and asks "What's wrong?" and "What could be better?"

2) Checks the conditions of utilities: water, sewer, gas, electric, and street lights. Are they working right? Can they work better?

3) Comes up with ideas and uses math and science to figure out how to use different technology to make those ideas real

4) Draws construction plans (blueprints)

5) Shares those plans with construction companies and chooses a company to do the work

Then finally, construction starts!
Would you like to be a civil engineer someday?